choice, thriving from one to another, May God Bless you. May God give you to be free you to be and never ~ Tanya

Damaged But Not Broken

How God Brings Restoration After Domestic Violence

By: Tanya Smith

Dedication

This book is dedicated first and foremost to my children (Jaleesa, JR, Leona, Jasmine and Tanesha) who have lived these experiences with me. There are no words that can express how much I love you and all my grandkids. I know you have seen my pain and my struggles, and I am so blessed to have my "Five Heartbeats". To my parents, Robbie and Marie, my sister Crystal and my nephew Erick.

It is also dedicated to all the women who are in a domestic violence relationship, those who have survived but are still suffering and needing healing and to survivors needing encouragement. May God be your refuge and strength.

With all my love,

Tanya Smith

February 17, 1974 to January 11, 2020

In Loving Memory of Christopher King, a great friend and graphic designer of the book cover. We met in 1997, and through the years we didn't keep in touch thru all of them, but when we did it was like we never lost contact. As my heart is broken, I sit here feeling so blessed that we met. You are truly missed. My prayers will continue to lift your wife and daughters.

Contents

Introduction

This book is written for everyone who has experienced domestic violence. Because of my abuse God has brought ministry out of my pain. I am alive to tell my testimony and bring awareness and healing to others that have and have walked and are still walking in my shoes. My heart aches when I hear the cries and battles of my sisters. I know that together we can prevail.

The Bible tells us that God takes all our bad and makes it good. (Romans 8:28, *"And we know that all things work together for good to them that love God, to them that are called according to His purpose."* It's these things that not only does He get the glory for, but the things that makes us who we are and how we can use these things in our personal ministries to help build the kingdom.

The chapters written in this book are my life accounts of the damage that domestic violence had on my life and how God delivered me through both of my abusive relationships. (Romans 8:37 says, "*Nay, in all things we are more than conquerors through Him that loved us*.") It tells not only that I have been restored and healed, but how God uses my experiences for His glory. It also describes what domestic violence is, how long it has been going on, how God can bring healing with His word, through counseling and treatments and how you can help.

By the end of this book I pray you see God's power through His Word to bring deliverance and restoration to your life or anyone you know in a domestic abuse relationship.

Chapter 1

In The Beginning

A Real Man Never Hurts A Woman
Be very careful when you make
a woman cry. Because God counts her
tears. The woman came out of a man's
rib. Not from his feet to be walked on.
Not from his head to be superior. But
from his side to be equal. Under the
arm to be protected. And next to
the heart to be loved. - Author Unknown

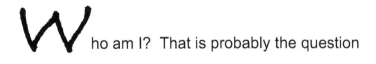

ho am I? That is probably the question

you are asking yourself. So, in this chapter I am going to tell you about me, my family, my childhood and how I became a survivor.

I was born March 19, 1973 to Robert and Lillian Smith of South Carolina. My Daddy is a Vietnam Veteran with the Marine Corps and became an instrument control and electronic engineer for a nuclear power plant in North Carolina for forty-seven years until he retired in 2018. My Mama is the backbone of the family. She is a stay at home Mom of two girls. As I finally grew up, I realized how hard of a job this really was.

My family was raised in a Southern Baptist Church where my paternal grandparents were a Deacon (until he passed away) and Sunday School teacher until she was too old to teach, but still helped in the classes till she passed away. Their love for the Lord was carried down through their children and grandchildren. Unfortunately, I don't remember my grandfathers on either side. My paternal grandfather passed when I was around two years old and my maternal grandfather passed away before my Mom was an adult. My paternal grandmother passed away in 2018 and I always knew she was praying for me. It was the literal meaning of "a praying grandmother". My maternal grandmother passed when I was eighteen. She was the glue that held the family together. When she passed, even family Christmas's weren't the same. Some of the family just stopped coming around or participating in Christmas. What I do remember most about her was I spent a few weeks every summer with her in South Carolina. I remember us walking down the country road picking up glass soda bottles and taking them to the store on the corner for money!

I grew up in a small beach town off the south-east coast of North Carolina. I love the water and even tried surfing once! I am a great swimmer and have taught my kids and one of my granddaughters how to swim.

I was the tomboy of the family. So, I played softball from the fifth grade thru the eleventh grade playing second base except for the first year or two. I also played basketball from the sixth grade to the eleventh grade as a shooting guard. I remember my parents didn't miss any of my games and my Daddy was even at most of my practices no matter what sport it was.

It was while playing softball in the fifth grade that I met one of my best friends, thirty plus years and we are still sisters! It was like both sides of our families "adopted" each other. Her, her sister and I all three played basketball and softball together from the time me and my best friend were in the fifth grade until her sister graduated a few years before us. It was through that friendship that my relationship with my sons' father was stronger. He was her sisters' best friend, so we saw each other a lot. Her sister is also a great friend and sister to me. My sons' father and I had hung out a few times right before summer break.

This leads us to the summer between my junior and senior year I got pregnant with my son. This was when my life started to change. I had moved out of my parents' house for a while and stayed at a friend's house. (Looking back now I realize that I was the rebellious teenager and eventually my Dad talked me into coming back home.) My sons father and I dated for about three months before I got pregnant and we broke up when I was four months pregnant because he decided he wanted to be back with his old girlfriend, who then also got pregnant and my son and his sister are four months apart. (Interestingly my son also has a sister three months older than him that I found out about not too long after she was born.)

This takes us into my senior year of high school. It was a few months before graduation and even though we were no longer together and barely spoke at all, there was an incident when I was still pregnant. There were about 30 or so of my classmates that were at a get together at a classmate's house. We were just hanging out as a sort of last class party before graduation. We left the classmates house to go to a club about 25 minutes away. I drove with my best friend and another one of our friends in my car. The group of us stopped to get gas before leaving to go to the club. I remember seeing a classmate of mines shotgun hanging in the back of his pickup truck. I didn't realize then how important that would be later that night.

We pulled up at the club and I never got out the car. I set in the parking lot. Most of the people I went with didn't go inside, they were just hanging around outside anyway. As I was sitting in my car with the window down talking to others outside, my sons father came up out of nowhere and snatched open the car door and tried to pull me out the car. He was yelling and trying to hit me telling me I needed to go home. (interesting because he was pulling me out the car while telling me I needed to leave.) He was drunk of course. One of my classmates ran up and grabbed him telling him to leave me alone, I wasn't even in the club, wasn't drinking and it was none of his business anyway. My sons father kept fighting with him trying to get to me, until that same classmate pulled out his shotgun and told my sons father if he didn't leave me alone, he would shoot him. That ended his rampage that night and should have been a sign for what was to come.

After my son was born, I moved back out and in with his father. I guess it is here where my domestic violence history really started. I only let this abuse happen once when my son was about a year old. We were driving to Baltimore to see some of his family when he got angry because two of our friends were supposed to come with us and decided at the last minute not to come. He stopped in the middle of the road and started beating me in my head. By the time I got to Baltimore I had knots in my head. I guess you could call this relationship puppy love, because it didn't take but a few weeks after that for me to move back home with my parents.

A year later I ran into a guy I had met when I was fourteen years old where we had worked at the same restaurant on the waterfront. God he was the most handsome, built and sexiest man I had ever seen! From that day, I fell head over heels in love with him. He spoiled me rotten. Even though he was the first love of my life, he also ended up the worst case of my domestic violence history.

Chapter 2

The Fight to Live

The beginning was August 1992 when I started

dating my daughters' father when I was nineteen years old.

I fell madly in love with him. I loved his big kind heart, the

love and attention he gave me. We did almost everything

together. He spoiled me and always made me feel like a

million dollars. Unfortunately, the alcohol and drug use

would change that loving, kind heart-ed man that I loved so

much into a monster. During the wonderful times there was the abuse. I stayed for many years, because I knew he wasn't always this person. I loved him so much that I was blinded by it. I seriously thought that he would change, and I could help him do that. Through the next six years and five months, I was physically, sexually, emotionally and mentally abused. I can recall several of the abusive times in detail. There are, I am sure, plenty that I have unconsciously blocked out.

March 19, 1993 was the first time. It was mine and my two-year-old sons' birthday. My boyfriend wasn't the father of my son so myself and his biological father threw him a party at Pizza Hut. My boyfriend didn't attend. My son's father needed a ride home from the party, so I took him. I didn't think it was a big deal at the time. I had no feelings for my son's father left. We were over. We stopped at a local gas station for gas and my boyfriend shows up. This was the first day of many abusive days to come. In the parking lot of the gas station he started to beat me until my son's father jumps out the car after him. (As you saw in chapter one how this made no since my sons' father was the first person to every hit me.) By the time the police showed up, I had to hide my bruises so the police wouldn't arrest him. You see, I loved him, he was drunk and promised it would never happen again.

Sometime before May 1994, he did it at least twice that I can remember in detail. This one night I was at the pool hall looking for him. I just knew he was with someone else, and he was. I was talking in front of the pool hall with his best friend trying to find out where he was. He walked up and I guess his guilty conscious got the best of him, and he started accusing me of wanting his best friend. He started hitting and shoving me. We left the pool hall walking to his mothers and he proceeded to hit me and pushed me down. I had always fought back, this time breaking his jaw.

May 8, 1994, we had our first daughter and moved to Greensboro, NC where our best friends had moved. Away from my family the abuse got worse along with his use of drugs. There were many nights between 1994 and 1996 that I thought I would go to sleep and I would wake up because I couldn't breathe. His hands were choking me as I slept. I tried going to a local organization for help and getting a restraining order, but in those days without physical marks or verbal threats to kill me, there was nothing they would do. So now I am too scared to just leave.

I am going to take a moment here to explain something. One of my best friends and the lady who edited my book for me, asked me to explain the "how he tried to kill me" in more detail. I think these next two quotes from books explain it better than I can, because I don't remember a lot about the incidents. Sherri Mabry Gordon wrote in her book, *Violence Against – Woman and Society;* "One narrowing example of physical violence is strangulation. Research shows a link between strangulation and the likelihood of domestic homicide. Woman who are strangled by a partner are seven times more likely to become the victims of a homicide or attempted homicide by that partner. Writes Kate Manne in the New York Times." [1] Rachel Louise Snyder states in her book, *What We Don't Know About Domestic Violence Can Kill Us*; "Strangulation is much more significant marker than a punch or a kick. 60% of domestic violence victims are strangled at some point during an abusive relationship, often repeatedly over years. Those strangled to the point of losing consciousness are at their highest risk of dying in the first 24-48 hours after the incident from strokes, blood clots, or aspiration. Domestic Violence victims are not routinely screened for strangulation or brain injury in the emergency rooms, and the victims themselves, who tend to have poor recall of the incident,

---

1   Gordan, 31

are often not even aware that they've lost consciousness."[2] This paragraph will also explain my reactions in the chapter 4 and my PTSD in chapter 5.

I had a miscarriage in late 1995. June 1996, I got pregnant with our second daughter. The day of the abuse that sticks out in my head here was the time I was pregnant with her and he beat me all over the kitchen. Slamming me into the stove and refrigerator until his baby sister jumped in and fought him. My daughter is a miracle to have made it through the abuse to being born.

Now back in our hometown late in 1996, I'm living with friend till we once again get our own place. I was there maybe a month and a half. You would think that while I am living away from him, I wouldn't go back. But once again, I loved him, even got him into rehab. Well rehab didn't last. Right after my daughter was born January 14, 1997, we moved back in together. I just knew he would get the help

---

2   Snyder, 65,66

he needed, and we would have a happy life together raising our children. This included my son. My boyfriend treated him like he was his own son. My son called him daddy before our oldest daughter was even born. My boyfriend spent a lot of time with my son and always took him places for father son time.

Early 1998, I am now praying for God to remove me from this situation safely and have either of us look back. I was raised in the church but like most teens I rebelled. Knowing who God was, I sought for Him to deliver me out of this mess. Suddenly, the lights got cut off and the rent was past due causing us to have to find somewhere to live. God answered my prayers, I had my way out, this time I wasn't looking back. He went to his mothers and I went to stay at a friend's house in Whiteville, NC.

Ten months later my best friend in Greensboro calls me and wants me to move in with her. I went I did. Three months later I got my own place. I would take the kids to see him in our hometown on the weekends. This one weekend his oldest sister told me he was going to die or go to jail if he stayed there and I was the only one that could help him.

May 1998 against my doubts, his oldest sister convinced me to take him to Greensboro so that He could get his life together. She told me I was the only one who could save him. She said he would be dead of in jail if he stayed. I was dating someone at the time, and I told him, this was a temporary situation because his kids needed him to get his life together and be stable. At this point we were just friends and out of the goodness of my heart I was trying to help him. He understood I had moved on with my life and was in love with the guy I was dating; and that him and I were just friends. On June 14, 1998 on a Tuesday evening and his birthday, it was the last straw for me. He came in from hanging out with a few friends and he lost it on me. He threw me around, hit me, and kicked the fan down the hallway, etc. I finally ran outside, and he locked me out keeping the kids inside. Finally, he calmed down enough to let me back in.

The next morning, I left like I normally did to go to work and take the kids to daycare, but instead I dropped the kids off and went to the courthouse to sign a 50B (restraining order). All the judges were in a conference till Thursday. I went back to the daycare and picked up the kids and left to head to Whiteville to my friend's house till Thursday with just the clothes on our backs. I had explained to my daycare provider what was going on when I picked the kids up because they would be out the rest of the week. She called me the next day and stated that my "boyfriend" had called them and the police because he was worried. When the police contacted her and she explained, the officer went back and told my "boyfriend" that we were fine, and I didn't want to be found. On Thursday I headed back to Greensboro to sign the 50B and the police evicted him from the house. I was able to go get some clothes. Still

scared I went back to my friend's house till Friday and then

home to my parents for the night. For the first time I told my

parents everything from 1992 – 1998. They couldn't believe

it. On Saturday morning my parents and I drove back to

Greensboro with some more of my stuff to move into the

new house. (Because I had not finished moving all of my

stuff from storage in my hometown yet.)

> Psalms 46:1 *"God is our refuge and
> strength, a very present help in trouble."*

Now watch how God moved on this day for my

benefit. When we got to Raleigh, NC on I40 my tire blows.

I did a few 360 degree turns in the middle of the interstate.

I remember as we are spinning around, looking at my two

daughters in the back seat, praying for God to save us. I

also looked at my parents in their truck behind me with my

son. Thinking, "Daddy please give me room!" If you know

I40 in Raleigh, then you know the traffic is always really

bad. The car stopped two feet from hitting a guard rail.

When the car finally stopped my parents got out the car and a off duty highway patrol officer. The officer and my Daddy said I had handled the car so well and they had no idea how I didn't hit the guard rail or another car. God had saved us from a terrible accident.

We went into Raleigh and got my tire fixed, then back on the road to finish the trip to Greensboro. When we pulled up and I hesitated to get out of the car. My dad asked me what was wrong. I said, "He's been here". There was a pile of my clothes in the yard, three trash cans on the porch. As we walked to them, they all smelled of gasoline. My dad goes inside first and he had destroyed everything I owned. He broke all my trophies, pictures, and cut up all my shoes outside of pouring gasoline my clothes. He left only the kids' room untouched. You see if it had not been for my tire blowing out, we would have gotten to the house while he was still inside. God not only saved me from an accident, but everything truly happens for a reason, because He also saved me from running into my kids' father at the house. We called the sheriff and when he got there, he told my parents that if they didn't get me out of there, he would kill me, that this was the worst case of domestic violence he had seen.

From my house I went into a shelter in Greensboro until we went to court for a permanent restraining order. The judge said we should seek marriage counseling. I couldn't believe it, not only were we not together anymore, we were never married. At the end of the hearing he told me he would kill me and whoever I was with. This time his threats didn't work. I decided then and there that I would not let him control me and the rest of my life. I made the decision to move to Fayetteville to be closer to my boyfriend. He knew everything that had happened before him and understood why I had tried to help my ex get on his feet for the kids. I requested that the shelter in Greensboro move me to a shelter in Fayetteville, NC, where they helped me in 24 hours get my own apartment and within 3 days a job. I spent 14 months in this program going through counseling for me and my kids.

Unfortunately, that relationship only lasted through early 2000. Later in 2000 I moved back to Greensboro with the man I had become to know as my best friend and who in 2001 became my husband number one, but that's another book. I thought I was ready to move back but I wasn't. For at least the next two to three years I was scared, paranoid, and didn't want to leave the house. I just knew I would run into him.

When we got to Greensboro, I found a psychiatrist, why I was never diagnosed with PTSD then I don't know. It could have saved a lot of grieve in my marriage. They were no help at all.

One beautiful Saturday in July of 2001, three months before we were married, there was a knock on our apartment door. There stood a married couple who were ministers evangelizing and inviting people to come to church. The next day, I got up and took the kids to church. That day changed my life forever. The next Sunday my boyfriend went. October 20, 2001 we were married.

During the first year in Greensboro and the first three years or our marriage I was struggling so bad emotionally. I was scared to go to work, I just didn't want to leave the house. I knew he would find me. What if I ran into him? I had to make sure the schools didn't post any pictures of the kids online, on TV or in the Newspaper. I had to explain to the schools why I didn't want any pictures published. I would walk into a store and people would probably think I was casing it because I was constantly looking over my shoulder and looking around at everyone. It upset my husband because his thought process was that it didn't matter if we ran into him, he could protect me. It never was that I didn't think he could or would protect me, it was just the fear of the unknown and how it would all play out.

There were the sleepless nights or better yet, we were laying in the bed and I had to rock myself back and forth until I finally fell asleep because I would still wake up scared about reliving his hands being wrapped around my neck. That really drove my husband crazy!

I know there is probably so much more he could probably say here. But the truth is I was so emotionally in a bad place, that some of it is a blur. I know that if it had not been for the love and support, and God, we would not have made it through.

Now with no self-confidence or self-esteem and very insecure in who I was, God starts His restoration process to build a confidant woman. A woman damaged but not broken. Below is the process of how I found "Tanya" and was able to move on.

Chapter 3

Restoration Begins

*Psa 23:1-6 "¹A Psalm of David. The LORD is my shepherd; I shall not want. ²He maketh me to lie down in green pastures: he leadeth me beside the still waters." ³**He restoreth my soul**: he leadeth me in the paths of righteousness for his name's sake. ⁴Yea, though I walk through the valley of the shadow of death, I will fear no evil: for thou art with me; thy rod and thy staff they comfort me. ⁵Thou preparest a table before me in the presence of mine enemies: thou anointest my head with oil; my cup runneth over. ⁶Surely goodness and mercy shall follow me all the days of my life: and I will dwell in the house of the LORD for ever."*

It took a lot of prayer, faith and self-examination for

God to restore me from this abuse. Because of no self-confidence or self-esteem, I was hard on myself and very negative about everything including myself. I was always thinking that other people were putting me down, when really, they were trying to help me. Sarah Jakes Roberts states in her book *Don't Settle for Safe*, "Your life was manifested because of a need that existed in the world. Feelings of unworthiness don't just damage our relationships; they diminish our ability to maximize the power available to us through our divine connection with God." You see even through all the therapy; I was still damaged. I had no idea who I was. I had a lot of built up pain and hurt that I had covered with a bandage in order to move forward with life. Telling myself I was a survivor and now that I was out of that relationship everything was great. But I had to realize that not only did I need to be healed from the hurt and pain, but I needed to find out who Tanya really was. I was in the church where healing can be made manifested because Jesus is the ultimate healer.

God took me through the Bible to find out who He said I was and that I was healed, and victorious. Here are a few verses that He took me to. I know that they will bring the same confidence and healing to you.

Who Am I

> Genesis 1:26, *"And God said, Let us make man in our image, after our likeness: and let them* **have dominion** *over the fish of the sea, and over the fowl of the air, and over the cattle, and over all the earth, and over every creeping thing that creepeth upon the earth."*

> Deuteronomy 28:13, *"And the LORD shall make* **thee the head, and not the tail; and thou shalt be above only, and thou shalt not be beneath***; if that thou hearken unto the commandments of the LORD thy God, which I command thee this day, to observe and to do them:"*

> Deuteronomy 28:3, *"Blessed shalt thou be in the city, and blessed shalt thou be in the field."*

1Peter 2:9, *"**But ye are a chosen generation, a royal priesthood, an holy nation, a peculiar people**; that ye should shew forth the praises of him who hath called you out of darkness into his marvellous light:"*

Luke 4:18, *"**The Spirit of the Lord is upon me**, because he hath **anointed me** to preach the gospel to the poor; he hath sent me to heal the brokenhearted, to preach deliverance to the captives, and recovering of sight to the blind, to set at liberty them that are bruised,"*

Luke 10:19, *"Behold, **I give unto you power** to tread on serpents and scorpions, and over all the power of the enemy: and nothing shall by any means hurt you."*

Mathew 22:14, *"For many are called, but few are chosen."*

Andrew Wommack in his book *Lessons from David: How to be a Giant Killer* states: "You are a King and Priest on the inside. You are a Son of God. You're anointed. You're powerful. One third of you is "wall-to-wall" Holy Ghost! Don't let other people's opinions and evaluations of who you are in the natural realm limit you!"

Victorious

Romans 8:37, *"Nay, in all these things we are **more than conquerors** through him that loved us."*

Ephesians 6:11-18, *"[11]Put on the whole armour of God, that ye may be able to stand against the wiles of the devil. [12]For we wrestle not against flesh and blood, but against principalities, against powers, against the rulers of the darkness of this world, against spiritual wickedness in high places. [13]Wherefore take unto you the whole armour of God, that ye may be able to withstand in the evil day, and having done all, to stand. [14]Stand therefore, having your loins girt about with truth, and having on the breastplate of righteousness; [15]And your feet shod with the preparation of the gospel of peace; [16]Above all, taking the shield of faith, wherewith ye shall be able to quench all the fiery darts of the wicked. [17]And take the helmet of salvation, and the sword of the Spirit, which is the word of God: [18]Praying always with all prayer and supplication in the Spirit, and watching thereunto with all perseverance and supplication for all saints;"*

Healing

1Peter 2:24, *"Who his own self bare our sins in his own body on the tree, that we, being dead to sins, should live unto righteousness: by **whose stripes ye were healed**."*

My favorite verse of them all 1 John 4:4, *"...For greater is He that is in me than he that is in the world."* My other favorite is Psalms 34:19, *"Many are the afflictions of the righteous: but the LORD delivereth him out of them all."*

I would confess these verses daily until I knew them and believed them in my heart. Along with these verses I had a "theme song" that I would play repeatedly that helped in my healing. It was Bishop T.D. Jakes featuring Shirley Murdock, "The Lady, Her Lover, and Lord."

Some people may not understand this, but during my restoration process, I would lay in bed in the mornings crying because of the pain and hurt I was reliving in order to get my healing. I would look out the window and see the face of Jesus in the trees. This was confirmation for me that everything was going to be alright, that I was alright. Many times, I would be sitting, crying and praying and I would feel God's hand resting on my head. I still feel this today as I have gone through more "bad things". This was my confirmation that He is with me always. For His Word says in Hebrews 13:5, *".....for he hath said, I will never leave thee, nor forsake thee."*

The restoration and healing did not come over night or in a few days or even in a few months. But one thing I did know was that God is able and it is all in His timing. I had to speak out loud every day, "I forgive _____". I had to speak this until it was manifested in my heart. Because in order for God to forgive me of my sins, I had to forgive my abuser. (Matthew 6:15, *"But if ye forgive not men their trespasses, neither will your Father forgive your trespasses."*) This forgiveness was tested. In 2002, God gave me a vision that I would have to tell the man that tried to kill me that I forgave him. I told God I couldn't do it, but He said, "yes you can." In April 2005, this came to reality. I was four months into my bachelor's degree, when in between classes my cell phone rang. It was his baby sister telling me that he wanted to speak with me. I called him, full of boldness and confidence. When we were on the phone, he apologized in a way that I had never heard him apologize before. For the first time it felt sincere and from his heart. I told him it was okay and that I forgave him, and that God still loves him. Then I told him "thank you". He couldn't understand my forgiveness and really couldn't grasp me telling him thank you. I told him, "all you put me through and everything you did to me, brought me to my knees. It made me the woman of God I am today and for that I thank you." This was the hardest conversation I had ever had in my life up to this point.

He still lived in Atlanta from 2002 or 2003 until 2018 when he moved back to our hometown. I have seen him six times since 1998. Once at his brother's funeral in 2002, on the Fourth of July in our hometown in 2010, and at our grandson's funeral in 2012. In 2016 we were at our granddaughter's birthday party and later in 2019 at our daughter's wedding. We also saw each other in July 2019, and we get along great. It took many years and true forgiveness. We have had conversations on the phone about our girls and I can speak to him without feeling all that hurt and pain. I minister to him when I can, because after all he is a lost soul.

I thought after this restoration process that this was the worst thing I could face. But there was more to come.

Chapter 4

The Choice to Live

You never imagine that you will have to go

through the same thing over again. I thought that once I

had learned to move on from my abuse there would never

come a time when it would happen again. How could I let

myself fall for that again? I mean, I own a foundation for

women of domestic violence. I am preaching and teaching

the Word of God. I do a conference called "Damaged but

not Broken". But in 2013 I started down that same path after a divorce from my first husband that left me so lost and once again broken.

In 2013 I thought I had met the right man. He was ten years older than me, that meant he was mature right? He had a good job; he was stable and seemed like he just had it all together. When we moved in together, I should have known it was a disaster waiting to happen. But after my divorce I was looking for someone to love me. Notice the first mistake was moving in together before we were married. I was already out of the Will of God.

In the beginning, it was him just drinking too much. Those nights he would come in and he would call me every name in the book and even talked about guns and shooting up people that weren't even in the house. I just ignored it and would talk to him when he was sober about his drinking and about how the enemy uses those moments in time where he has no control over himself to come into his mind.

Brad Steiger states the same thing in his book, *Real Vampires, Night Stalkers and Creatures from the Darkside*. He states, "far too many (people) use alcohol and drugs in order to put themselves into a relaxed state – which very often deteriorates into a drunken or a drugged stupor. Alcohol and drugs leave the user wide open to spirit parasites."

This time I never let it get as bad as before. But there were a few times that it could have been worse. The physical abuse started in 2016 when he came in drunk and pushed me. I went to the hospital the next morning because my chest was hurting so bad, I couldn't breathe, my left arm was going numb, my neck and shoulder were hurting. The ER said they couldn't find anything. They released me. A few days later I was back. Both times I was sent in an ambulance from my job. They still couldn't find anything. I ended up at my primary care's office and spent three months trying to find out what was wrong. I had an ultrasound to check for ulcers, a heart doctor to make sure I hadn't had a stroke or heart attack or any other heart related problems, a endoscopy and colonoscopy, and a diagnostic breast examine, until I finally asked for a full body CAT Scan. Finally, the CAT Scan showed that my C3 and C5 discs in my neck were bulging and herniated. I spent twelve weeks in physical therapy and six months of taking three steroid injections in the top of my back and a total of eight months taking medication that had steroids in them and gave me some short-term memory loss issues. Fast forward to 2018, then it was throwing bags of clothes at me, and full water bottles. Still a lot of name calling and pushing. Till the night he came in and grab me by my throat and slammed me down. That was the last straw. This happened in October 2018 and I spent the next four months getting myself ready to move out. Luckily for me my job has a domestic violence organization with in it for employees that helped me. They paid for my first month's rent, deposit and lights. They also gave me other resources to help me get on my feet. I moved out January 30, 2019. It was not an easy process, especially financially getting on my feet by myself. July 29, 2019, I realized I couldn't continue to try and handle the emotion and mental issues that I was having. I really thought I could handle it on my own. I went out of work on short term disability. I started counseling and therapy August 2019. It has been rougher this time I think because it also brought up a lot of what happened to me in my past. My fears are back, can't sleep, anxiety off the charts and finally someone diagnosed me with PTSD. I read up on it after the diagnoses and realized that I should have been diagnosed in the early 2000s because I was suffering from all the signs.

It is now into 2020 and I am still going through the process of the financial stress and therapy for my PTSD.

I am also asking myself, is there a pattern that I missed, a pattern that caused me to be in more than one abusive relationship. Per the website www.*escapeabuse.com* if you have been in one of more abusive relationships then you may want to look at some of the possible reasons.

Have you ever asked yourself if maybe unconsciously you are picking partners who are in some ways similar to an abusive, neglectful, or emotionally absent parent because that's what you're comfortable with or find most "exciting"?

You can't make an abuser stop being angry and controlling, and abusers rarely change. But you can work towards understanding yourself better so that you will not "need" to be loved or accepted by another person so badly that you will tolerate being abused by them out of fear of being considered unlovable, fear of abandonment, or fear of rejection.

In other words, the type of people and relationships you may tend to gravitate towards or that "excite" you might not be good ones for you. Your mission is to find out why

you might gravitate towards unhealthy relationships or

abusive types of people.

Chapter 5

The Battle of PTSD

P er the American Psychiatric Association the

definition is "Post-traumatic stress disorder (PTSD) is a

psychiatric disorder that can occur in people who have

experienced or witnessed a traumatic event such as a

natural disaster, a serious accident, a terrorist act,

war/combat, rape or other violent personal assault."

"PTSD has been known by many names in the past, such as "shell shock" during the years of World War I and "combat fatigue" after World War II. But PTSD does not just happen to combat veterans. PTSD can occur in all people, in people of any ethnicity, nationality or culture, and any age. PTSD affects approximately 3.5 percent of U.S. adults, and an estimated one in 11 people will be diagnosed PTSD in their lifetime. Women are twice as likely as men to have PTSD."[3]

"People with PTSD have intense, disturbing thoughts and feelings related to their experience that last long after the traumatic event has ended. They may relive the event through flashbacks or nightmares; they may feel sadness, fear or anger; and they may feel detached or estranged from other people. People with PTSD may avoid situations or people that remind them of the traumatic event, and they

---

3   American Psychiatric Association

may have strong negative reactions to something as ordinary as a loud noise or an accidental touch."[4]

"A diagnosis of PTSD requires exposure to an upsetting traumatic event. However, exposure could be indirect rather than firsthand. For example, PTSD could occur in an individual learning about the violent death of a close family. It can also occur as a result of repeated exposure to horrible details of trauma such as police officers exposed to details of child abuse cases."[5]

"Victims of violence who develop PTSD may startle easily, feel tense of on edge, have difficulty sleeping, or have anger outbursts. 54-84% of battered women suffer from PTSD, 63-77% experience depression and 38-75% suffer from anxiety according to the Florida Coalition Against Domestic Violence.

---

4   American Psychiatric Association

5   American Psychiatric Association

Per Lindsey Wyskowski in her book, *Living with PTSD*, she tells us that people cope in different ways. "Coping mechanisms differ from person to person. When someone is trying to process how they feel, it is not uncommon to feel upset and scared, dwell on what happened, and be unable to sleep or concentrate. The events can cause people to lose their appetite, be numb to the world, or even feel nothing at all."[6] She also states that "because people different, PTSD looks different for everyone who is battling the condition. No one person experiences it the same way."[7] "For people living with PTSD, intrusive memories can be one of the more challenging symptoms to overcome in part because they return unpredictably. Seth Gillihan, a PTSD researcher says, "part of the haunting quality of PTSD is that these memories live with us. The memory can come up uninvited without any obvious triggers and these memories will just

---

6   Wyskowski, 13
7   Wyskoski,16

run through as your mind tries to process and make sense of them.""[8]

The hippo-campus portion of the brain manages our memories. For those suffering from PTSD, the amygdala portion becomes more prominent. It controls our fears and strong emotions. When it becomes the prominent portion, it gives us the fight-or-flight response.

My Story

It took the second abuse for me to be diagnosed with PTSD. However, when I look at all the symptoms, I had all of these in the early 2000s. If my husband (at the time) and I would have known this, it may have made the first several years of our relationship and marriage easier. I remember a specific event while we were standing in the bathroom at my apartment when we were dating, and he had just affectionately put his around my shoulder and neck. In a split-second reaction I elbowed him as hard as I could in the

---

8   Wyskoski, 29

ribs. You see that touch brought back the flashback and feelings of being choked. I also remember the fears of going to sleep at night where I would have to literally rock myself to sleep. Per Wyskoski, nightmares are common for survivors. I know for me I have memories and then I have nightmares. I think even some of my memories are played out in my dreams as nightmares. Charles Marmar, a psychiatrist and director of the PTSD research program in New York University's Langone Medical Center states, "Nightmares can be like a movie, or they can even be weird dreams in which the event you witnessed gets morphed in certain ways."[9]

I am sure he can tell many stories of those first years and what I was going through and how difficult it was for me but for him also. He would always tell me to stop putting myself down and being so negative.

---

9   Wyskoski, 31

Through finishing my book, which actually has been therapeutic for me, I have been in therapy with a counselor and seeing a psychiatrist to help me with my PTSD. It is nothing to be ashamed of. If you are having any of these symptoms, please reach out for help. Your primary care physician can be a good place to start. Build a support system. It was hard for me to let my kids and family know what I was dealing with, but I had to realize that it wasn't my fault and I needed them. I can honestly say that I am still in therapy and I am still healing. Remember you never have to face any of this alone.

Short-Term Disability Failed Me

Along with my seeking help for my PTSD I went out on Short-term Disability through my job. I will not name the insurance company due to legalities, but I am going to tell this horror story to bring you awareness so that I pray you will never have to go through this yourself. It is hard enough to deal with the abuse, then the PTSD, anxiety, fears and depression then must deal with the added anxiety that a failed system in our insurance causes.

It all started out great. I went out on leave and the first 45 days my short-term disability paperwork was signed by my primary care physician. After the first 45 days it had to be signed by a psychiatrist. The "psychiatrist" that I made an appointment with ended up not being a psychiatrist, but a counselor. I was already seeing a counselor through my benefits with my job through my medical insurance with Aetna. I was allowed six free visits. So, at the last minute, before my paperwork had to be turned in, I had to find another psychiatrist. Well I found one. The very first visit she diagnosed me with PTSD (which my counselor had already advised that I had). She then put me on medication and said she would see me in two weeks. Two weeks later she is filling out my disability paperwork the whole visit. She did not know how to fill out the paperwork and kept asking me how to fill it out. Well I didn't know how to fill it out. To make a long story short, she contradicted herself on the paperwork. In one question is stated that I couldn't function at work and on the next question stated I could. But she also didn't want to give them a return to work date because she didn't know how long it would take for my therapy to have me ready to go back to work. It could be 120 days or longer is what she verbally told me. The disability company kept asking her for more information until she just text me that she would not fill out anymore paperwork for them and she would no longer see me.

The disability company then said they could take my care information from my counselor since she was actively seeing me. This all started in October when due to my psychiatrist, my case was denied and then went into appeal. I have now been appealing since October 2019 to currently in January 2020. My counselor has been sending in information almost monthly and they keep denying asking her for more information. Per my counselor the paperwork from the disability company that is being sent back to her is basically stating that since I am not suicidal that I am not serious enough to miss work. It doesn't matter about my fears, my depression, or anxiety that barely allows me to get off the couch. It takes everything out of me to try and see my counselor and to write all this down to get my book published.

So as of Monday January 6, 2020, I had to quit my job of six years to take out my 401K to pay my rent up because I almost got evicted November 2019 because I was not getting paid my short-term disability. I am in the process of my truck getting repossessed, my lights have been cut off numerous times and I barely have one meal a day. I have been going to the plasma center to try and get food, gas and put money on my lights. December of 2019, I reached out to my jobs Employee Assistance program and they paid my November and December rent so that I wouldn't get evicted. However, they will not do that again. Instead now I am currently looking for an attorney to sue the disability company.

This is just another example that the system is still failing us a domestic violence survivor. Not only do I have my normal fears and anxiety, I have PTSD and can't seem to get any help. I had to stop seeing my counselor and couldn't see another psychiatrist because I wasn't getting paid in order to pay them. This has been a complete nightmare. When we need help and can't seem to get it and the benefits, we think we have failed us, where do we turn?

The Symptoms

The American Psychiatric Association explains that the symptoms can be put into four categories and can vary in severity.

1. **Intrusive thoughts** such as repeated, involuntary memories; distressing dreams; or flashbacks of the traumatic event. Flashbacks may be so vivid that

people feel they are re-living the traumatic experience or seeing it before their eyes.

2. **Avoiding reminders** of the traumatic event may include avoiding people, places, activities, objects and situations that bring on distressing memories. People may try to avoid remembering or thinking about the traumatic event. They may resist talking about what happened or how they feel about it.

3. **Negative thoughts and feelings** may include ongoing and distorted beliefs about oneself or others (e.g., "I am bad," "No one can be trusted"); ongoing fear, horror, anger, guilt or shame; much less interest in activities previously enjoyed; or feeling detached or estranged from others.

4. **Arousal and reactive symptoms** may include being irritable and having angry outbursts; behaving recklessly or in a self-destructive way; being easily startled; or having problems concentrating or sleeping.

Changes in Emotional Reactions:

⚐ Overwhelming guilt or shame
⚐ Jumpiness – being easily startled or frightened – jumping out of your skin
⚐ Sleep disturbances
⚐ Difficulty concentrating
⚐ Always in "defense" mode – on guard for danger
⚐ Irritability
⚐ Angry outburst
⚐ Aggressive behavior
⚐ Self-destructive behavior (e.g., reckless driving, substance abuse)

Negative Changes in Thinking and Mood:

⚐ Feeling negatively about yourself and others

⅄ Lack of interest in activities you once found enjoyment in
⅄ Difficulty maintaining relationships with others
⅄ Memory problems – not being able to remember parts of the traumatic event
⅄ Feelings of hopelessness for the future (e.g., marriage, career, living a normal life span)
⅄ Emotional numbness – feeling detached from others
⅄ Inability to experience positive emotions

Reactions to PTSD include:

⅄ driving to fast
⅄ drinking excessively
⅄ self-harming
⅄ thoughts/acts of suicide
⅄ self-harm

Chapter 6

Picking up the Pieces

Picking up the pieces of your life is not an easy

process. But it can be done with support, prayer and help from God. The way we pick up the pieces is different for everyone. It can be to move to a different city or state. It can be a new job or going back to school. It all has to do with making a different and better life for you and your children, if you have any. Just remember that you are not alone, and you can do it. You are a strong intelligent woman. For me my picking up the pieces of my life were through working in the ministry. Here's how He worked to help me pick up my pieces.

Out Came Ministry

> "When God calls us, it is a very big deal. It is holy ground. It produces within us such a reverence and awe that it is hard to know what to do with ourselves."[10]

> "Calls are essentially questions. They aren't questions you necessarily answer outright; they are questions to which you need to respond, expose yourself, and kneel before. You don't want an answer you can put in a box and set on a shelf. You want a chariot to carry you across the breadth of your life."[11]

As you remember in the ending of chapter two, I found the Lord and got married. This story picks up where that chapter left off.

---

10 Barton, 74
11 Barton, 84

About 1 ½ years later, I was prophesied by several ministers that I had a ministry for women and would be a powerful mouthpiece for the Lord. During this time frame I had to learn who I was. I had been damaged mentally and emotionally. I had low self-esteem and self-respect. A woman who used to be so confident in who she was, when she met this abuser that in the process had somewhere and somehow lost herself. "In our day it is easy to dismiss the idea of calling as a mere concept, but God called to Moses, out of the burning bush saying (in effect), "I know the question about your identity has been a little confusing for you, but I have always known who you are. In the very essence of your being, you are someone .... Now that you know who you are, I am calling you to do something out of your being."[12]   God restored me so that I can be a blessing and a living testimony to others. I stand before women today knowing that God can restore your self-

---

12 Barton, 73

esteem, self-respect, love, outlook on life, and bring healing and full restoration to you. I know that what I went through was not for Tanya, but God took all my bad and made it good so that I can minister to others about how wonderful He is and how much He loves us. Today I am a living testimony, just a vessel and mouthpiece that God uses to bring Him glory and to restore those that I meet. I love the Lord with all my soul and spirit. He is truly my everything. I can't go a second of any day without Him. The scripture that blessed me the most when I got saved was 1John 4:4 "...*greater is He that is in me than he that is in the world.*" This scripture is a representation of how I was restored because I knew that He was in me and if He was in me, there was nothing the enemy could do to get me down. I now tread over Satan and keep him under my feet. I know now that I am always victorious, and I win every battle. God was always with me in that painful part of my life. He always had His hand upon my life, and He knew that there would come a day when I would step out in my call to bring

Him honor and glory. I would have the opportunity to tell

my story and show thru it all, He was right there with me.

> Ephesians 4:11-13a [11]"*And he gave some, apostles; and some, prophets; and some, evangelists; and some, pastors and teachers;* [12]*For the perfecting of the saints, for the work of the ministry, for the edifying of the body of Christ:* [13a]*Till we all come in the unity of the faith, and of the knowledge of the Son of God,"*

Because of my call to ministry and my life

experiences and testimony, I have started Rejuvenated

Women's Foundation. Out of my hurt and pain, and God's

love and restoration power, this ministry will enhance

women to realize that they are someone special. This

outreach will help empower women to know that they can

survive and that they have options to make it out of their

domestic violence situation. I have started the 'Damaged

but not Broken Conference' to spread the word that we are

survivors and that no matter what God love us and wants to bless us.

May 2007, I graduated from John Wesley Bible College with my Bachelor's in Pastoral Ministries with a minor in Theology and Counseling. I graduated from Shaw University Divinity School receiving my Master of Divinity in 2013 and I was on staff at Moses Cone Health System as a Volunteer Chaplain. I taught the Associates Degree for the North Carolina School of Theology for two years as an Elder at New Birth Sounds of Thunder Christian Center under Apostle H. Sheldon McCray in 2011 and 2012.

> Luke 4:18 *"The Spirit of the Lord is upon me, because he hath anointed me to preach the gospel to the poor; he hath sent me to heal the brokenhearted, to preach deliverance to the captives, and recovering of sight to the blind, to set at liberty them that are bruised, [19]To preach the acceptable year of the Lord."*

In 2013 I moved to Jacksonville Florida. While ministry has not been as detailed since the move, I am currently getting my Doctoral Degree in Ministry from The Kings University in Southlake, Texas. I am looking to go back into teaching Biblical Studies and Theology to undergrad students, while pursuing my dream to write books and articles. I will continue the call to preach God's Word and run RWF (Rejuvenated Women's Foundation) and run the Damaged but Not Broken Conferences across the United States.

God has been faithful through it all and continues to be faithful through all my delays and distractions. He delivered and restored me, and I pray that He will use this book to deliver and restore you.

Chapter 7

What is Domestic Violence

Per the National Domestic Violence Hotline

website defines domestic violence as "Domestic violence (also called intimate partner violence (IPV), domestic abuse or relationship abuse) is a pattern of behaviors used by one partner to maintain power and control over another partner in an intimate relationship."

They also state that "Domestic violence does not discriminate. Anyone of any race, age, sexual orientation, religion or gender can be a victim – or perpetrator – of domestic violence. It can happen to people who are married, living together or who are dating. It affects people of all socioeconomic backgrounds and education levels. Domestic violence includes behaviors that physically harm, arouse fear, prevent a partner from doing what they wish or force them to behave in ways they do not want. It includes the use of physical and sexual violence, threats and intimidation, emotional abuse and economic deprivation. Many of these different forms of domestic violence/abuse can be occurring at any one time within the same intimate relationship."

Battery

Domestic Violence is also known as battery. Battery is defined by Dawn D Matthews in her book "*Domestic Violence Sourcebook*" "it can be emotional, economic, sexual, using children, threats, using male privilege, intimidation, isolation, and other behaviors to bring fear, intimidation and to show power/control." (Matthews, pg. 15)

There are three categories that acts of domestic violence fall into. These acts can fall into one or more of these categories:

- ⚔ Physical Battering is the physical attack from bruising to murder. They tend to start out as small or trivial events that escalate to more frequent and more serious.
- ⚔ Sexual Abuse is sexual violence wherein the woman is forced to have sex or do unwanted sexual activities.

- ⚔ Psychological Battering includes constant verbal abuse, harassment, excessive possessiveness, isolating her from friends and family, deprivation of resources and destruction of personal property.

Domestic violence is not just physical harm and battery. It also includes marital rape, emotional, mental and verbal abuse.

12 Myths About Domestic Violence

1. It's only domestic violence if there's physical assault.

   False. Domestic violence includes a lot of controlling

behaviors that can be physical, emotional, psychological, sexual, or financial.

2. Domestic violence is a matter of the home.

   False. It happens at home or in public to people who are married, living together, dating or separated.

3. Victims are responsible for what happens to them.

   Definitely not. Victims don't deserve and are never asking for it. No human being deserves this treatment. No one deserves to be beaten, raped, controlled, degraded or humiliated.

4. Domestic violence happens because of poverty or lack of education.

   False. There is no specific person domestic violence happens to. I personally have a master's degree and a good job, so it doesn't have any age, ethnicity, financial status, or educational background.

5. Domestic violence happens because men can't control their anger.

   False. Abuse is a pattern. It's always there, men just seen to hide who they are. It's never a breaking point.

6. Domestic violence is a woman's issue.

   Sort of. It does happen to men as well; about 1 out of 9. It is more common in women though, about 1 out of 3.

7. People lie about being abused.

   Rarely. There may be a small amount who claim being abused for personal gain, it is very rare. It takes a lot of courage to report domestic violence. People should always believe they are telling the truth. When people disbelief them, they are likely to not seek help. This leads women to distrust the police and not report what has happened.

8. Good people can't be abusive.

   False. Abusers can very charming, intelligent, and loving when they want to be. They are masters of deceit.

9. Victims of domestic violence are powerless.

   False. Victims feel helpless that is true. The abuser makes them feel that way.

10. Leaving a domestic violence is easy.

   False. Victims are afraid of what the abusers will do to them or their loved ones. Victims can be financially dependent on them. There may be a fear of losing custody of their children, fear of homelessness, lack of support, and even hope that the abuser will change.

11. Once a survivor escapes her abuser, everything's rainbows and sunshine.

   False. Lots of victims end up going back to their abusers more than once. The first time I was abused, I went back several times, for several different reasons.

Even after a successful move she still needs help rebuilding her life and recovering from the trauma.

12. There's nothing we can do to help.

Wrong. There are things that you can do to help them. First, you can listen without judgment, offer them a place to stay, help them find resources and validate their feelings.

Domestic abuse is a complex and largely hidden

phenomenon. The consequences of domestic violence are

far-reaching and have a significant effect on the long-term

health and emotional well-being of those affected.

Chapter 8

Domestic Violence History

I n this chapter I am going to focus on three eras in

life. I think that it is important for you to see how long

domestic violence has been in existence. This is not a 21st

century ideal that has just started. It has been around a

long time and it is time for us to make the appropriate

changes to save the lives of these women. We are

important, we are beautiful and made in the image of God.

So, we are going to start with the Biblical references, then to two thousand years ago, then the 18th Century History and lastly bringing us to a time-line from the 1800s into the 2000s.

Biblical References

The story of Tamar is one that I know we are all familiar with. But I am including it here because it shows that violence is not a new thing. It has happened for centuries and even before Christ. This does not make it a good thing, nor does it make it right. What it does show is that there needs to be something done. Women die for no reason at the hands of the men that state that they love us and will protect us, or at the hands of men who just want to show they are powerful and in control.

> **2Samuel 13:1** *"And it came to pass after this, that Absalom the son of David had a fair sister, whose name was Tamar; and Amnon the son of David loved her."*

So from here we know that Amnon desired his sister Tamar so his friend and cousin Jonadab advised him to lay in the bed and pretend to be sick and when his father David

came in to check on him, he asked his father if Tamar could

come take care of him. David went to Tamar and advised

her to go cook for her brother. We pick up f at verse 10.

> *2Samuel 13:10 "And Amnon said*
> *unto Tamar, Bring the meat into*
> *the chamber, that I may eat of*
> *thine hand. And Tamar took the*
> *cakes which she had made, and*
> *brought them into the chamber to*
> *Amnon her brother. 11 And when*
> *she had brought them unto him*
> *to eat, he took hold of her, and*
> *said unto her, Come lie with me,*
> *my sister. 12 And she answered*
> *him, Nay, my brother, do not*
> *force me; for no such thing ought*
> *to be done in Israel: do not thou*
> *this folly. 13 And I, whither shall I*
> *cause my shame to go? and as*
> *for thee, thou shalt be as one of*
> *the fools in Israel. Now therefore,*
> *I pray thee, speak unto the king;*
> *for he will not withhold me from*
> *thee. 14 Howbeit he would not*
> *hearken unto her voice: but,*
> *being stronger than she, forced*
> *her, and lay with her."*

Now that Amnon had gotten what he had desired

from his sister, he hated her. She was confused and hurt, I believe, because she then tells him that him rejecting her was worse than his initial act of violation of her. He has her kicked out and the door bolted behind her. Tamar then tore her clothes that were the symbol of royalty and being a virgin, put ashes on her head and went crying. We know that her brother Absalom hated Amnon and David was very angry.

> *2Samuel 13:21 "But when king David heard of all these things, he was very wroth. 22 And Absalom spake unto his brother Amnon neither good nor bad: for Absalom hated Amnon, because he had forced his sister Tamar."*

Two years later Absalom kills Amnon.
Another act of violence comes from

Judges 19, called Gibeah's Crime.

> *Judges 19:22 "Now as they were making their hearts merry, behold, the men of the city, certain sons of Belial, beset the house round about, and beat at the door, and spake to the master of the house, the old man, saying, Bring forth the man that came into thine house, that we*

may know him. [23] *And the man, the master of the house, went out unto them, and said unto them, Nay, my brethren, nay, I pray you, do not so wickedly; seeing that this man is come into mine house, do not this folly.* [24] *Behold, here is my daughter a maiden, and his concubine; them I will bring out now, and humble ye them, and do with them what seemeth good unto you: but unto this man do not so vile a thing.* [25] *But the men would not hearken to him: so the man took his concubine, and brought her forth unto them; and they knew her, and abused her all the night until the morning: and when the day began to spring, they let her go.* [26] *Then came the woman in the dawning of the day, and fell down at the door of the man's house where her lord was, till it was light.* [27] *And her lord rose up in the morning, and opened the doors of the house, and went out to go his way: and, behold, the woman his concubine was fallen down at the door of the house, and her hands were upon the threshold.* [28] *And he said unto her, Up, and let us be going. But none answered. Then the man took her up upon an ass, and the man rose up, and gat him unto*

his place. ^{29} *And when he was*
come into his house, he took a
knife, and laid hold on his
concubine, and divided her,
together with her bones, into
twelve pieces, and sent her into
all the coasts of Israel."

People don't understand why he would cut up her body into twelve pieces and send a piece to the twelve tribes of Israel. Matthew Henry's Complete Commentary states that he wanted to "confirm the truth of the story and to affect them more with it." He hoped that someone would join him in punishing these men for what they had done. So in essence he cut her body up and sent it to the twelve tribes for a dramatic effect.

Two Thousand Years Ago

In the 1st Century, Egnatius Metellus took a cudgel and beat his wife to death because she had drunk some wine. He was not blamed or charged. Because there were laws of sobriety, it was considered a good example of justice for woman who violated the laws. It was against the law for any woman to get drunk on wine. They stated that it "closes the door on all virtues and opens it to vices". [13]

Per Wikipedia, domestic abuse was recorded in history only when it was done by the powerful and influential men. The Emperor Nero subjected his first wife Claudia Octavia to torture and had even sent her to prison. Later it was said that he had her killed then married his pregnant mistress Poppawa Sabina. He later kicked her to death for criticizing him. However, it is also told by some that she died in childbirth or by having a miscarriage. Lastly we have Commodus who was thought to have also killed his wife and his sister.

Eighteenth Century Domestic Violence [14]

The story of Mary Eleanor Bowes, Countess of Strathmore is a domestic violence story that has made

---

[13]
http://zimmer.csufresno.edu/~mariterel/hist129t_sp'04_roman_law_se lections.htm

[14] www.wondersandmarvels.com/2009/03/18th-century domestic-violence.html

history. You see in 18th Century England it was considered normal for a man to beat his wife, so Mary's story became a great win for victims of domestic violence.

In England the husbands were legally entitled to beat their wives in order to "correct" their conduct in moderation. Francis Buller, the judge, stated in court that a husband could beat his wife with a stick as long as it was no thicker than his thumb.

However, the domestic abuse against Mary was extreme. She was beaten with sticks, candlesticks and whips. Her husband tore her hair out, burned her face and even threatened her with knives.

After eight years of abuse she filed for divorce on the grounds of adultery and cruelty. Her claim was also backed by the house servants who saw everything that had taken place to her.

Her husband kidnapped her before a decision was made on the case. He held her for eight days he threatened her with a pistol and rape. When she was

rescued, she won her divorce case through two appeals.

She reclaimed her property and children. He then spent

the rest of his life in prison.

The Timeline

- 1871 – Alabama is the first state to rescind man's legal right to beat their wives.

- 1967 – One of the United States first woman's shelters for domestic violence opens in Maine.

- 1978 – Both the National Coalition Against Sexual Assault and the National Coalition Against Domestic Violence are formed in the United States.

- 1984 – The United States Congress passes the Family Violence Prevention Services Act. (The FVPSA supports lifesaving services including emergency shelters, crisis hotlines, counseling, and programs for undeserved communities throughout the United States, American Indian and Alaska Native communities, and territories. It is administered by the U.S. Department of Health and Human Service and is the only federal funding source dedicated to domestic violence shelters and programs.)

- 1985 – The United States Surgeon General identifies domestic violence as a public health issue.

- 1996 – The VAWA (The Violence Against Women

Act - is a landmark piece of legislation that sought to improve criminal justice and community-based responses to domestic violence, dating violence, sexual assault and stalking in the United States) funds the National Domestic Violence Hotline (800-799-SAFE) and takes its first call on February 21$^{st.}$ The first month they took almost 4,900 calls.

- 2009 – Barack Obama is the first President to declare April as Sexual Assault Awareness month.

Chapter 9

Know the Signs

Knowing the signs of domestic violence can

save your life or someone you love or know. Each of the

women that read this, this is for you. It's for you who don't

know you are even in an abusive relationship, or don't know

that the man you are dating is an abuser. This section is for

a friend or family member that needs to keep their eyes

open for their family members or friends that are in an

abusive relationship.

What is Abuse

- ⋏ Mistreat: treat badly
- ⋏ Pervert: change the inherent purpose or function of something
- ⋏ Maltreatment: cruel or inhumane treatment
- ⋏ use foul or abusive language towards
- ⋏ a rude expression intended to offend or hurt
- ⋏ use wrongly or improperly or excessively

Warning Signs of Domestic Violence (By: The National Domestic Violence Hotline)

One of the hardest things to determine in the beginning of a relationship is if it will become abusive.

"Most people seem just great in the early stages of a relationship. Possessive and controlling behaviors don't always appear overnight, but rather emerge and intensify as the relationship grows. Domestic violence doesn't look the same in every relationship because every relationship is different. But one thing most abusive relationships have in common is that the abusive partner does many kinds of things to have more power and control over their partner."

Violence against women jeopardizes their lives, bodies, psychological minds, integrity and freedom. It is called "the most pervasive yet least recognized human rights abuse in the world."

What is an Abusive Relationship?

When defining domestic violence, one typically refers to abuse in an intimate relationship. However, one must define "abuse" and "intimate".

Intimate Relationship: two people with emotional ties despite sexual orientation or relationship status. The two are well known to each other emotional ties are either past or present. There may be other ties as well.

Abusive Relationship: not only behavior but also the meaning to the behavior being acted out by the person involved and their intent.

What do people consider abusive?

It depends on intention or perpetrator, the effect of the victim, and if the nature of the behavior is repetitive. The incident is not unique, and pattern is where the abuser uses his or her power against the victim. However, be aware that if it's the first time, 99% of the time, it will not be the last. There is no reason why any man should beat a woman. Remember there is no excuse.

How do you know if you are being abused?

Red Flags: experiencing fear with partner, feels unsafe at home, physically injured, partner control's person's actions, speech, and/or relationships.

Maintaining power and control over partner is the essence of domestic violence. When on leaves it threatens their control and evokes greater violence.

Does your partner:
- Embarrass or make fun of you in front of others
- Put down your accomplishments or goals
- Make you feel like you are unable to make decisions
- Use intimidation or threats to gain compliance
- Tell you that you are nothing without them

- Treat you roughly – grab, push, pinch, shove or hit you
- Call you several times a night or show up to make sure you are where you said you would be
- Use drugs or alcohol as an excuse for saying hurtful things or abusing you
- Pressure you sexually for things you aren't ready for
- Make you feel like there is no way out of the relationship

Do you:
- Sometimes feel scared of how your partner will act
- Consistently make excuses to other people for your partner's behavior
- Believe you can help your partner change if you only change something about yourself
- Try not to do anything that would cause conflict or make your partner angry
- Feel like no matter what you do, your partner is never happy with you
- Always do what your partner wants you to do instead of what you want
- Stay with your partner because you are afraid of what your partner would do if you broke up

When it comes to why men batter women, they usually do it to make the woman do what he wants her to do. There are two characteristics of male batterers. The

87

first one is they may have witnessed abuse as a child. The second is chronic alcohol abuse.

Recognizing Abusive Personalities

As women we not only want to but need to know what the behaviors and personalities of abusive men are. Here's a list of ten behaviors or personalities that will help.[15]

- Jealousy – it is a sign of lack of trust and possessiveness.

- Controlling Behavior – abusers tend to be angry when we are late coming back home.

- Quick Involvement – married, engaged or living together six months after knowing them does not give enough time to know someone.

- Unrealistic Expectations – abusers expect women to meet all their needs.

- Isolation – abusers try to cut her off from all resources.

- Blames others for problems – if he is always unemployed, he blames her for him not keeping a job.

---

15 Matthews, 219

- Playful use of force in sex – he may like to to throw her down or hold her down during sex.

- Verbal Abuse – they say things that are meant to be cruel and hurtful. They like to use cursing, mimicking, and repetition to degrade her, in a tone of voice that is threatening.

- Past Battering – a big sign is if he has a

  history of domestic violence.

- Threats of violence – they may threaten to kill you, break your neck, slap that smile off your face, etc.

Why Stay:

You may ask why people stay. There are external

reasons and internal reasons

External: lack of housing, religious, lack of support

Internal: desire to maintain household wish to preserve the relationship between the children and other parent, feeling responsible for partner's welfare, and love for partner.

Sometimes the cost of leaving outweighs the benefits of abuse.
Here are six detailed reason of why women stay.

1. Love – You love them. They can be so loving and caring at

times. Sometimes those moments are even more often than the abuse. However, you have to realize that the abuse is not safe or healthy and that outweighs the loving and caring times.

2. Hope – hope that they will change. Hope that with time they will grow up from childish things.

3. Children – you may have children together and you do not want them to grow up in a broken home.

4. Embarrassment and Shame – you could be embarrassed or ashamed that you "let" this happen to you.

5. Financial Dependence – you cannot financially make it on your own.

6. Fear – They may threaten to kill you, your family, or to take away your children from you.

Things to Do and Don't Do for you to help[16]

Do:

- Ask
- Express concern
- Listen and validate
- Offer help
- Support her decisions

Don't:
- Wait for her to come to you
- Judge or blame
- Pressure her
- Give advice
- Place conditions on your support

People don't really understand or realize that leaving an abusive relationship is often the most dangerous time. Abuse is about the abuser having control and power of the victim, so when she leaves, she is taking that away from him. It is taking away the threats he makes over her, making him want to retaliate against her in order to maintain his control and power over her. When she leaves the risk of death or serious injury increases.

---

16 Matthews, 255

Chapter 10

Statistics

When it comes to the statistics, most people

have no idea what they are. People normally don't look at them unless they are professionals helping survivors, or researchers, and maybe the victims themselves. I wanted to add them to my book so that anyone who reads my story will see them. If you don't know how bad a situation is, then how can you help.

National Statistics (www.ncadv.org/statistics)

⚔ On average, nearly 20 people per minute are physically abused by an intimate partner in the United States. For one year, this equates to more than 10 million women and men.

⚔ 1 in 4 women and 1 in 9 men experience severe intimate partner physical violence, intimate partner contact sexual violence, and/or intimate partner stalking with impacts such as injury, fearfulness, post-traumatic stress disorder, use of victim services, contraction of sexually transmitted diseases, etc.

⚔ 1 in 3 women and 1 in 4 men have experienced some form of physical violence by an intimate partner. This includes a range of behaviors (e.g. slapping, shoving, pushing) and in some cases might not be considered "domestic violence."

⚔ 1 in 7 women and 1 in 25 men have been injured by an intimate partner.
⚔ 1 in 10 women have been raped by an intimate partner. Data is unavailable on male victims.

⚔ 1 in 4 women and 1 in 7 men have been victims of severe physical violence (e.g. beating, burning, strangling) by an intimate partner in their lifetime.

⚔ 1 in 7 women and 1 in 18 men have been stalked by an intimate partner during their lifetime to the point in which they felt very fearful or believed that they or someone close to them would be harmed or killed.

⚔ On a typical day, there are more than 20,000 phone calls placed to domestic violence hotlines nationwide.

⚔ The presence of a gun in a domestic violence situation increases the risk of homicide by 500%.

⚔ Intimate partner violence accounts for 15% of all violent crime.

⚔ Women between the ages of 18-24 are most abused by an intimate partner.

⚔ 19% of domestic violence involves a weapon.

⚔ Domestic victimization is correlated with a higher rate of depression and suicidal behavior.

⚔ Only 34% of people who are injured by intimate partners receive medical care for their injuries.

Rape:

⚔ 1 in 5 women and 1 in 71 men in the United States has been raped in their lifetime.

⚔ Almost half of female (46.7%) and male (44.9%) victims of rape in the United States were raped by an acquaintance. Of these, 45.4% of female rape victims and 29% of male rape victims were raped by an intimate partner.

Stalking:

⚔ 19.3 million women and 5.1 million men in the United States have been stalked in their lifetime. 60.8% of female stalking victims and 43.5% men reported being stalked by a current or former intimate partner.

Homicide:

⚔ A study of intimate partner homicides found that 20% of victims were not the intimate partners themselves, but family members, friends, neighbors, persons who intervened, law enforcement responders, or bystanders.

⚔ 72% of all murder-suicides involve an intimate partner; 94% of the victims of these murder suicides are female.

Children of Domestic Violence:

⚔ 1 in 15 children are exposed to intimate partner violence each year, and 90% of these children are eyewitnesses to this violence.

Economic Impact:

⚔ Victims of intimate partner violence lose a total of 8.0 million days of paid work each year.

⚔ The cost of intimate partner violence exceeds $8.3 billion per year.

⅄ Between 21-60% of victims of intimate partner violence lose their jobs due to reasons stemming from the abuse.

⅄ Between 2003 and 2008, 142 women were murdered in their workplace by their abuser, 78% of women killed in the workplace during this timeframe.

Physical/Mental Impact:

⅄ Women abused by their intimate partners are more vulnerable to contracting HIV or other STI's due to forced intercourse or prolonged exposure to stress.

⅄ Studies suggest that there is a relationship between intimate partner violence and depression and suicidal behavior.

⅄ Physical, mental, and sexual and reproductive health effects have been linked with intimate partner violence including adolescent pregnancy, unintended pregnancy in general, miscarriage, stillbirth, intrauterine hemorrhage, nutritional deficiency, abdominal pain and other gastrointestinal problems, neurological disorders, chronic pain, disability, anxiety and post-traumatic stress disorder (PTSD), as well as noncommunicable diseases such as hypertension, cancer and cardiovascular diseases. Victims of domestic violence are also at higher risk for developing addictions to alcohol, tobacco, or drugs.

Chapter 11

Counseling and Treatment

When it comes to counseling and treatment,

there are so many people that don't know what to do or
what to say. I have been in therapy and it is very hard to
find someone who understands and knows what to say. It
is one of those instances where if you have not been there,
it can be hard to understand and help someone in a
domestic violence relationship.

In Peter Breggin's Book *Guilt, Shame and Anxiety* he states that there are three steps to emotional freedom. They are:[17]

1. Identify your negative legacy emotions;

2. Reject any compliance with these emotions; and

3. Triumph over and transcend these emotions.

Breggin also tells us that "guilt, shame, and anxiety are so painful that we will do almost anything to ward them off. To avoid feeling guilt we make no choices that seem remotely bad, selfish, or self-serving. To avoid feeling anxiety we give up taking risks or trying anything new or different."[18]

Domestic Violence

Power and Control Wheel (By: Lenore Walker, 1980)

The important thing to understand about identifying abuse is not just learning to watch for particular behaviors but being aware of how behavior is functioning.

---

17   Breggin, 123
18 Breggin, 125

The core component of abuse is the misuse of power to control another person. This dynamic manifest itself in many ways from the very extreme and obvious to the very sublime. The behaviors vary, but the goal remains the same: to gain, maintain, or regain control. Consider the varieties of abusive behaviors in this "power and control wheel."

PTSD

When it comes to treating PTSD is better to get help early after the event to lessen the severity of later symptoms. Unfortunately, this was not the case for me. Twenty-one years later and after the second abuse, I am not just getting the help I need. It seems that there are people, including my short-term disability company, that do not understand that my feelings and emotions, fears and anxiety are so powerful that I can function some days and other days, I cannot function including not getting out the bed. There are good days and there are bad days. However, if the disability companies know that there are good days, then that is all they see. If I am not suicidal, then I am okay and can function. It is a very hard diagnosis to have that is still so misunderstood.

Treatments (www.psycom.net/post-traumatic-stress-disorder/#treatment)

Several types of treatment options are available if you are suffering from post-traumatic stress disorder. The most often prescribed method of treatment is psychotherapy. Medications and other types of physical treatment options are also prescribed. Your doctor will formulate the best treatment course of action for you.

Psychotherapy: often referred to as "talk therapy" has been shown to elicit great responses from sufferers of post-traumatic stress disorder. Cognitive therapy is focused on recognizing patterns of thinking that get you "stuck" in your emotional state. For example, this type of therapy might help you in recognizing cognitive patterns associated with negative perceptions of normal situations. Exposure therapy is often coupled with cognitive therapy if you have been diagnosed with PTSD. Exposure therapy focuses on safe exposure to what is causing you intense fear. This exposure enables you to cope with the stimulus effectively and rationally. Eye movement desensitization and reprocessing (EMDR) is a form of therapy that combines exposure therapy with guided eye movements. These combination of events in EMDR help you in your cognitive processing of traumatic events and allow you to effectively change your reactions to these types of events.

Medications: that have been found useful in the treatment of post-traumatic stress disorder include antidepressants and anti-anxiety medications. Selective serotonin reuptake inhibitors (SSRIs), including Zoloft and Praxil, have been approved by the Food and Drug Administration as antidepressant treatments for PTSD.

Anti-anxiety medications are typically prescribed short-term to relieve severe anxiety problems associated with PTSD. They are usually only prescribed temporarily because of the ease of addiction to this type of medication. Nightmare suppressant drugs (e.g., Prazosin) may also be prescribed if you are suffering from post-traumatic stress disorder to help you sleep more easily and with fewer disruptions.

Therapy Includes:

- ⋏ Finding a therapist that has a background in treating PTSD

- ⋏ CBT (Cognitive Behavioral Therapy) – to change thoughts of the trauma

- ⋏ PE (Prolonged Exposure Therapy) – face the memories and scenarios that caused the stress or fear gradually.

- ⋏ EMDR (Eye Movement Desensitization and Reprocessing) – modifying the way people feel, think, and remember the event or events.

- ⋏ Animals – especially dogs can ease the pain of people living with PTSD. "Emotional support and service dogs are especially helpful to people who have sustained abuse, assault, or trauma involving another person, all of which can negatively affect victims ability to trust others."[19] My dog Onyx is registered as an Emotional Support Dog and a Service Dog. I am looking into getting his training done. Some people don't

19 Breggin, 62

understand why I take him everywhere with me, but to me he is my peace. I can always count on him and when there are days that I can't get out of bed, I know I at least have to get up to feed and walk him. He even helps me with a sense of purpose. Someone to love and care for.

Christian Counseling

When it comes to Christian counseling there has to b a balance between Christianity and psychology. We know that Christianity is where we believe that Jesus is the Messiah and He died and rose again for our sins, so we walk each day trying to be more like Him. Being more like Him means that we look at things differently than people who do not believe in God and Jesus. There are ways that we do things as well as how we react to and see things. When it comes to psychology, we must find out why a person reacts to things the way they do.

Psychology is defined as the science that studies mental, behavioral and relational processes, both normal and pathological. Per Larry Crabb in his book *Effective Biblical Counseling*, he states that, "if psychology offers insights that will sharpen our counseling skills and increase our effectiveness, then we want to know them."[20]

Christian counseling should provide us with spiritual, emotional, mental support using Biblical principles without being judgmental. In my studies I have had to take both psychology classes and Christian counseling classes for my minor in counseling. For us to be effective, we must know and study psychology not just the Bible and we have to know how to use them together. We must watch those lines and be able to effectively have them co-exist. If we don't then we can cause more damage than good. We should also never take the holier than thou approach. We are to show Christ through the counseling. Not use judgment and force Christ and the Christian lifestyle on anyone. Crabb also states that "Christian counselors must be sensitive to the depths of selfishness resident within human nature. Our goal is maturity: to become more like

---

20 Crabb, 21

God."[21] He goes on to say that "maturity involves two elements: (1) immediate obedience in specific situations and (2) long-range character growth."[22] I do believe that these things do come with maturity in God, but if we are counseling someone who is not a Christian, then we cannot expect these things to have bearings on our counseling. Once again, we can only show Christ does not force Him. We must understand that everyone who seeks us for counseling may not already know God, but they have tried everything else and they are still seeking for help to heal. We must remember that we don't heal, but He does. We are just the gateway or voice He uses to bring healing and deliverance.

In Stephen P Greggo's book *Counseling and Christianity* he states that, "counseling is an applied discipline that utilizes information and methods from various

---

21 Crabb, 15
22 Crabb, 15

sources. It can be succinctly defined as person-to-person dialogue to guide and support change."[23]

Here are a few diagrams that I found in Greggo's book that I thought would be beneficial. The Stages of Counseling[24] and Levels of Counseling[25].

Stages of Counseling

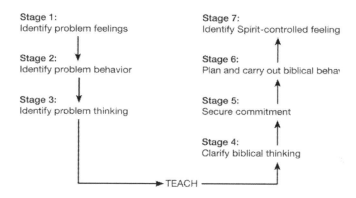

Levels of Counseling

Counseling by

Level I   Problem Feelings ———— ENCOURAGEMENT ——→ Biblical Feelings

Level II Problem Behaviors ———— EXHORTATION ———— → Biblical Behavior

Level III Problem Thinking ———— ENLIGHTENMENT ——→ Biblical Thinking

---

23 Greggo, 25
24 Greggo, 94
25 Greggo, 95

Just remember that when it comes to counseling, you need to be not just a Biblical Scholar or Pastor, you need to know how to counsel and in order to know that you then need to know psychology and the Bible for Biblical Counseling.

I have nothing against counseling outside of Biblical Counseling by any means. This is section is not stating that there is anything wrong with counselors and counseling that are not Biblical based, but this book is written with a Biblical foundation and therefore the need to discuss, to some extent, Biblical Counseling.

Chapter 12

Legal Rights

Legal rights differ from state to state. But there

are federal laws as well. It is very important that everyone

knows the laws, especially the ones that are state specific.

Each domestic violence coalition will have the laws per their

states. Here are just a few main points.

The Violence Against Women Act (VAWA)

The following information on VAWA is found at

www.family.findlaw.com. The Act was created in 1994 and

some additions were added in 1996. The Act outline grant

programs to prevent violence against women and created

the National Domestic Violence Hotline. New protections

were given to victims, the included confidentiality of new

address and changes to immigration law that allows a

battered spouse to apply for permanent residency.

Key provisions are:

⅄ Full funding of rape kits and
legal/court fees for domestic
violence protection orders
(retraining orders or orders for
protection are a legal directive
that orders individuals to avoid
any communication with his/her
partner for a specified period of
time. There are 2-3 million
issued every year in the United
States for domestic violence.[26])

---

26 Family Violence, 152

- Victim protection orders are recognized and enforced in all state, tribal and territorial jurisdictions within the United States.

- Implementation and funding of domestic violence crime units in local communities.

- Special domestic violence and sexual violence training for law enforcement officers.

- Ability of tribal courts to try non-Indian spouses or intimate partners of Indian women in domestic or dating violence cases.

- Provision allowing undocumented immigrants who are the victims of domestic violence to apply for a green card in exchange for helping law enforcement prosecute their abusers.

Section 922(g)[9] is the domestic violence misdemeanor law. It is when someone is convicted for a crime "committed by an intimate partner, parent, or guardian of the victim that required the use or attempted use of physical force or the threatened use of a deadly weapon."

Interstate traveling is also addressed. "A convicted abuser may not follow the victim into another state, nor may a convicted abuser force a victim to move to another state."

State Laws

When it comes to state domestic violence laws there are differences. Differences range from the definition to the requirements under mandatory reporting laws. In some states medical professionals may have to report suspected abuse to the police. Because of these differences the whole process of escaping a domestic violence situation depends on the state in which the victim lives.

Most states have "adopted preferred policies that require police to either arrest one or both parties at the scene, or to write a report justifying why an arrest is not made."

Domestic violence laws also include mandatory reporting. This require medical professionals to report to the police when there is a reasonably suspected that there has been domestic violence. These laws are different between states. For instance, California states that "counselors and psychologists are not subject to mandatory reporting. It applies only to medical professionals who have provided medical services for physical conditions." This is to encourage victims to attend counseling sessions for their mental health, even if they're not ready to tell the police about the abuse. This is important to know because in the state of California medical professionals are subject to criminal punishment if they fail to report abuse. Per federal law the medical professional has to alert the victim that the report is being filled. There are only two states that don't mandate medical professionals to report abuse. They are New Jersey and Wyoming.

The following are examples of state arrest policies for domestic violence complaints:

⊼ California - Officer is encouraged to arrest where there's probable cause; must arrest for violations of domestic violence protective order; dual arrests are discouraged (but not prohibited); officer shall make reasonable effort to identity primary aggressor.

⊼ New York – Officer must arrest the perpetrator either when there's probable cause that they've committed a felony against a member of the household or when a protective order has been violated.

⊼ North Carolina - Officer may arrest the perpetrator when there's probably cause that they've committed a felony; a misdemeanor and they may cause injury or property damage unless they're arrested; or they've committed one of a specific lists of misdemeanors against a household member.

Chapter 13

Helpful Resources

Domestic Violence Awareness and resources

has come a long way from through time, even in the years

from the first time it happened to me. You may ask if that's

the case then why do we need more awareness? The truth

is that even though the resources are getting better and the laws have gotten better, it is still happening every day. There is some woman somewhere scared for her life from the man who swore to protect her and love her.

Studies suggest that women who experience intimate partner violence (IPV) carry the effects to their jobs. I know I did. I couldn't think or function and all I did was cry. The study also shows that victims "who reported the abuse caused them to be absent and tardy, to be less productive while at work, to lose advancement opportunities, to lose their jobs and to earn lower wages."[27] There are local organizations in almost every city in every state that can help with awareness, counseling, finances, legal advocates and some that provide shelters. There is also a list in this chapter of the National and State Domestic Violence Coalitions that can also offer help and advice, and even direct you to those shelters in your state.

There are also major companies as well as maybe

---

27 Family Violence, 176

some small companies that can also aid. I just happen to work for one of those major companies the second time this happened to me. I work for Merrill, a Bank of America Corporation (used to be Merrill Lynch until 2019). Bank of America is number eight on Fortune's annual "Change the World" list, which ranked 52 companies that positively impact the world in August 2019. I say all of that about the company I work for because without their help, I would not have been financially ready to leave when I needed to or get the free counseling I needed to assist with my PTSD. You see they have a department for domestic violence that gives us advice, puts us in contact with our local organization, they paid my deposit and first month's rent, light deposit, gave me money for food, gave me six free visits with a counselor, and gave me a list of apartments in the area and local food banks. Because I am not from Jacksonville, I had no idea where to turn. But when I reached out to my supervisor, she told me about the department. I had seen emails, but I thought they only gave awareness. Thank God, they do so much more.

I am not going to say that every company has the same benefits as mine, but I will say to find out if they do and what they do.

Safety Plans[28]

Making a safety plan is one of the biggest ways to save your life when you decide to leave. If you follow your plan, the outcome for you to leave without any issues will be greater than leaving without a plan. Below is some guidelines for a safety plan from womenslaw.org. Your plan does not have to be exactly like this one.

Plan for how you are going to leave, including where you're going to go, and how to cover your tracks. Make one plan for if you have time to prepare to leave the home. Make another plan for if you have to leave the home in a hurry.

28 Www.womenslaw.org

119

⅄If you can, keep any evidence of the physical abuse and take it with you when you leave. Make sure to keep this evidence in a safe place that the abuser will not find – this may mean that you must keep it in a locked drawer at work or with a trusted family member. If the abuser finds it, you could be in more danger. Such evidence of physical abuse might include:

⅄Pictures you have of bruises or other injuries. If possible, try to have these pictures dated;

⅄Torn or bloody clothing;

⅄Household objects that the abuser damaged or broke during a violent episode;

⅄Pictures that show your home destroyed or messed up after violence happened;

⅄Any records you have from doctors or the police that document the abuse;

⅄Whenever you are hurt, go to a doctor or to an emergency room as soon as possible if you can. Tell them what happened. Ask them to make a record of your visit and of what happened to you. Be sure to get a copy of the record.

⚔ A journal that you may have kept with details about the abuse, which could help prove the abuse in court.

⚔ Anything else you think could help show that you've been abused.

⚔ If you have evidence of other types of abuse (threatening voicemails, text messages, emails, etc.), bring copies of those with you as well.

⚔ Get a bag together that you can easily grab when you leave. Some things to include in the bag are:

⚔ Spare car keys;

⚔ Your driver's license;

⚔ A list of your credit cards so that you can track any activity on them;

⚔ Your checkbook;

⚔ Money;

⚔ Phone numbers for friends, relatives, doctors, schools, taxi services, and your local domestic violence organization;

⊼ A change of clothing for you and your children;

⊼ Any medication that you or your children usually take;

⊼ Copies of your children's birth certificates, Social Security cards, school records and immunizations;

⊼ Copies of legal documents for you and the abuser, such as Social Security cards, passports, green cards, medical records, insurance information, birth certificates, marriage license, wills, welfare identification information and copies of any court orders (such as your protection order or custody order);

⊼ Copies of financial documents for you and the abuser, such as pay stubs, bank account information, a list of credit cards you hold by yourself or together with the abuser;

⊼ Any evidence you've been collecting to show that you've been abused; and

⚔A few things you want to keep, like photographs, jewelry or other personal items.

⚔Hide this bag somewhere the abuser will not find it. Try to keep it at the home of a trusted friend or neighbor. Avoid using next-door neighbors, close family members, or mutual friends, as the abuser might be more likely to find it there. If you're in an emergency and need to get out right away, don't worry about gathering these things. While they're helpful to have, getting out safely should come first.

⚔Hide an extra set of car keys in a place you can get to easily in case the abuser takes the car keys to prevent you from leaving.

⚔Try to set money aside. If the abuser controls the household

⚔ money, this might mean that you can only save a few dollars per week; the most important thing is that you save whatever amount you can that will not tip off the abuser and put you in further danger. You can ask trusted friends or family members to hold money for you so that the abuser cannot find it and/or use it.

⚔If you have not worked outside of the home and worry about your ability to support yourself, try to get job skills by taking classes at a community college or a vocational school if you can. This may help you to get a job either before or after you leave so that you won't need to be financially dependent on the abuser.

⚑ Getting a protective order can be an important part of a safety plan when preparing to leave. Even if you get a protective order, you should still take other safety planning steps to keep yourself and your children safe. A legal protective order is not always enough to keep you safe. Locate your state in our Restraining Orders section to find out more information about getting a protective order.

⚑ Leave when the abuser will least expect it. This will give you more time to get away before the abuser realizes that you are gone.
⚑ If you have time to call the police before leaving, you can ask the police to escort you out of the house as you leave. You can also ask them to be "on call" while you're leaving, in case you need help. Not all police precincts will help you in these ways, but you may want to ask your local police station if they will.

⚑ If you have pets and you are worried about their safety and welfare if they were left behind, consider reading through the Animals & Family Violence section in the Animal Welfare Institute webpage. They provide information about this topic including safety planning for pets and including pets in protection orders.

If you plan on taking your children with you when you leave, it is generally best to talk to a lawyer who specializes in domestic violence and custody issues beforehand to make sure that you are not in danger of violating any court custody order you may have or any criminal parental kidnapping laws. This is especially true if you want to leave the state with the children. If you are considering leaving without your children, please talk to a lawyer who specializes in custody before doing this. Leaving your children with an abuser may negatively affect your chances of getting custody of them in court later.

If you are fleeing to a confidential location and you fear that the abuser will go looking for you, you might want to create a false trail after you leave. For example, you could call motels, real estate agencies, schools, etc., in a town at least six hours away from where you plan to go and ask them questions that will require them to call you back. Give them your old phone number (the number at the home

125

you shared with the abuser, not the number to the place you are going). However, do not make these phone calls before you leave. If anyone calls you back while you are still with the abuser, or if the abuser is able to check your phone to see what numbers you have called, the abuser would be tipped off that you are preparing to leave, which could put you in great danger.

The List of Coalitions

National Coalition for Domestic Violence

www.ncadv.org
600 Grant, Suite 750
Denver, Colorado 80203
303-839-1852

Coalitions by State (www.ncadv.org/state-coalitions)

Alabama Coalition Against Domestic Violence

1420 I-85 Parkway
Montgomery, AL 36101
(334) 832-4842 Fax: (334) 832-4803
(800) 650-6522 Hotline
Website: www.acadv.org
Email: info@acadv.org

Alaska Network on Domestic and Sexual Violence

130 Seward Street, Suite 214
Juneau, AK 99801
(907) 586-3650 Fax: (907) 463-4493
Website: www.andvsa.org
Email: andvsa@andvsa.org

Arizona Coalition to End Sexual and Domestic Violence

2800 N. Central Avenue, Suite 1570
Phoenix, AZ 85004
(602) 279-2900 Fax: (844) 252-3094
(800) 782-6400 Nationwide
Website: www.acesdv.org
Email: info@acesdv.org

Arkansas Coalition Against Domestic Violence

700 S. Rock Street
Little Rock, AR 72202
(501) 907-5612 Fax: (501) 907-5618
(800) 269-4668 Nationwide
Website: www.domesticpeace.com
Email: acadv@domesticpeace.com

California Partnership to End Domestic Violence

1107 9th Street, #910
Sacramento, CA 95812
(916) 444-7163 Fax: (916) 444-7165
(800) 524-4765 Nationwide

Website: www.cpedv.org
Email: info@cpedv.org

Colorado Coalition Against Domestic Violence

1330 Fox Street, Suite 3
PO Box 40328
Denver, CO 80203
(303) 831-9632 Fax: (303) 832-7067
(888) 778-7091
Website: www.ccadv.org
Email: info@ccadv.org

Connecticut Coalition Against Domestic Violence

912 Silas Deane Highway, Lower Level
Wethersfield, CT 06109
(860) 282-7899 Fax: (860) 282-7892
(888) 774-2900 In State DV Hotline
Website: www.ctcadv.org
Email: contactus@ctcadv.org

Delaware Coalition Against Domestic Violence

100 West 10th Street, Suite 903
Wilmington, DE 19801
(302) 658-2958 Fax: (302) 658-5049
(800) 701-0456 Statewide
Website: www.dcadv.org
Email: dcadvadmin@dcadv.org

DC Coalition Against Domestic Violence

5 Thomas Circle Northwest
Washington, DC 20005
(202) 299-1181 Fax: (202) 299-1193
Website: www.dccadv.org
Email: info@dccadv.org

Florida Coalition Against Domestic Violence

425 Office Plaza Drive
Tallahassee, FL 32301
(850) 425-2749 Fax: (850) 425-3091
(850) 621-4202 TDD
(800) 500-1119 In State
Website: www.fcadv.org

Georgia Coalition Against Domestic Violence

114 New Street, Suite B
Decatur, GA 30030
(404) 209-0280 Fax: (404) 766-3800
(800) 334-2836 Crisis Line
Website: www.gcadv.org
Email: info@gcadv.org

Hawaii State Coalition Against Domestic Violence

1164 Bishop Street, Suite 1609
Honolulu, HI 96813
(808) 832-9316 Fax: (808) 841-6028
Website: www.hscadv.org
Email: admin@hscadv.org

Idaho Coalition Against Sexual and Domestic Violence

Linen Building
1402 W. Grove Street
Boise, ID 83702
(208) 384-0419 Fax: (208) 331-0687
(888) 293-6118 Nationwide
Website: www.idvsa.org
Email: info@engagingvoices.org

Illinois Coalition Against Domestic Violence

806 South College Street
Springfield, IL 62704
(217) 789-2830 Fax: (217) 789-1939
(217) 242-0376 TTY
Website: www.ilcadv.org
Email: ilcadv@ilcadv.org

Indiana Coalition Against Domestic Violence

1915 West 18th Street, Suite B
Indianapolis, IN 46202
(317) 917-3685 Fax: (317) 917-3695
(800) 332-7385 In State
Website:www.icadvinc.org
Email: icadv@icadvinc.org

Iowa Coalition Against Domestic Violence

6200 Aurora Avenue, Suite 405E
Urbandale, IA 50322

(515) 244-8028 Fax: (515) 244-7417
(800) 942-0333 In State Hotline
Website: www.icadv.org
Email: icadv@icadv.org

Kansas Coalition Against Sexual and Domestic Violence

634 Southwest Harrison Street
Topeka, KS 66603
(785) 232-9784 Fax: (785) 266-1874
Website: www.kcsdv.org
Email: coalition@kcsdv.org

Kentucky Domestic Violence Association

111 Darby Shire Circle
Frankfort, KY 40601
(502) 209-5382 Phone Fax (502) 226-5382
Website:www.kdva.org
Email: info@kdva.org

Louisiana Coalition Against Domestic Violence

P.O. Box 77308
Baton Rouge, LA 70879
(225) 752-1296 Fax: (225) 751-8927
Website: www.lcadv.org
Email: info@lcadv.org

Maine Coalition To End Domestic Violence

One Weston Court, Box #2
Augusta, ME 04330
(207) 430-8334 Fax: (207) 430-8348
Website: www.mcedv.org
Email: info@MCADV.org

Maryland Network Against Domestic Violence

4601 Presidents Drive, Suite 370
Lanham, MD 20706
(301) 429-3601 Fax: (301) 809-0422
(800) 634-3577 Nationwide
Website: www.mnadv.org
Email: info@mnadv.org

Jane Doe, Inc./Massachusetts Coalition Against Sexual Assault and Domestic Violence

14 Beacon Street, Suite 507
Boston, MA 02108
(617) 248-0922 Fax: (617) 248-0902
(617) 263-2200 TTY/TDD
Website: www.janedoe.org
Email: info@janedoe.org

Michigan Coalition Against Domestic and Sexual Violence

3893 Okemos Road, Suite B-2
Okemos, MI 48864
(517) 347-7000 Phone/TTY Fax: (517) 248-0902

Website: www.mcedsv.org
Email: general@mcedsv.org

Minnesota Coalition For Battered Women

60 E. Plato Blvd., Suite 130
St. Paul, MN 55107
(651) 646-6177 Fax: (651) 646-1527
(651) 646-0994 Crisis Line
(800) 289-6177 Nationwide
Website: www.mcbw.org
Email: mcbw@mcbw.org

Mississippi Coalition Against Domestic Violence

P.O. Box 4703
Jackson, MS 39296
(601) 981-9196 Fax: (601) 981-2501
(800) 898-3234
Website: www.mcadv.org
Email: support@mcadv.org

Missouri Coalition Against Domestic and Sexual Violence

217 Oscar Drive, Suite A
Jefferson City, MO 65101
(573) 634-4161 Fax: (573) 636-3728
Website: www.mocadsv.org
Email: mocadsv@mocadsv.org

Montana Coalition Against Domestic & Sexual Violence

P.O. Box 818
Helena, MT 59624
(406) 443-7794 Fax: (406) 443-7818
(888) 404-7794 Nationwide
Website: www.mcadsv.com
Email: mtcoalition@mcadsv.com

Nebraska Domestic Violence Sexual Assault Coalition

245 S. 84th Street, Suite 200
Lincoln, NE 68510
(402) 476-6256 Fax: (402) 476-6806
(800) 876-6238 In State Hotline
(877) 215-0167 Spanish Hotline
Website: www.ndvsac.org
Email: help@ndvsac.org

Nevada Network Against Domestic Violence

250 South Rock BLVD., Suite 116
Reno, NV 89502
(775) 828-1115 Fax: (775) 828-9911
Website: www.nnadv.org
Email: info@nnadv.org

New Hampshire Coalition Against Domestic and Sexual Violence

P.O. Box 353
Concord, NH 03302
(603) 224-8893 Fax: (603) 228-6096
(866) 644-3574 In State
Website: www.nhcadsv.org
Email: info@nhcadsv.org

New Jersey Coalition for Battered Women

1670 Whitehorse Hamilton Square Road
Trenton, NJ 08690
(609) 584-8107 Fax: (609) 584-9750
(800) 572-7233 In State
Website: www.njcbw.org
Email: info@njcbw.org

New Mexico Coalition Against Domestic Violence

1210 Luisa Street, Suite 7
Mailing Address: 1000 Cordova Place, #52
Santa Fe, NM 87505
(505) 246-9240 Fax: (505) 246-9434
(800) 773-3645 In State
Website: www.nmcadv.org
Email: info@nmcadv.org

New York State Coalition Against Domestic Violence

119 Washington Avenue, Suite 12210
Albany, NY 12054
(518) 482-5464 Fax: (518) 482-3807
(800) 942-5465 English-In State
(800) 942-6908 Spanish-In State
Website: www.nyscadv.org
Email: nyscadv@nyscadv.org

North Carolina Coalition Against Domestic Violence

3710 University Drive, Suite 140
Durham, NC 27707
(919) 956-9124 Fax: (919) 682-1449
(888) 997-9124
Website: www.nccadv.org

North Dakota Council on Abused Women's Services

521 E. Main Avenue, Suite 250
Bismarck, ND 58501
(701) 255-6240 Fax: (701) 255-1904
(888) 255-6240 Nationwide
Website: www.ndcaws.org
Email: contact@cawsnorthdakota.org

Action Ohio Coalition For Battered Women

P.O. Box 423
Worthington, OH 43085
(614) 825-0551 Fax: (614) 825-0673
(888) 622-9315 In State
Website: www.actionohio.org
Email: actionohio@wowway.biz

Ohio Domestic Violence Network

1855 E. Dublin Granville Road
Columbus, OH 43229
(614) 781-9651 Fax: (614) 781-9652
(614) 781-9654 TTY
(800) 934-9840
Website: www.odvn.org
Email: info@odvn.org

**Oklahoma Coalition Against Domestic Violence
and Sexual Assault**

3815 North Santa Fe Avenue, Suite 124
Oklahoma City, OK 73118
(405) 524-0700 Fax: (405) 524-0711
Website: www.ocadvsa.org
Email: Prevention@ocadvsa.org

**Oregon Coalition Against Domestic and Sexual
Violence**

9570 SW Barbur Boulevard, Suite 214
Portland, OR 97219
(503) 230-1951 Fax: (503) 230-1973
(877) 230-1951
Website: www.ocadsv.com
Email: adminasst@ocadsv.com

**Pennsylvania Coalition Against Domestic
Violence**

3605 Vartan Way, Suite 101
Harrisburg, PA 17110
(717) 545-6400 Fax: (717) 545-9456
(800) 932-4632 Nationwide
Website: www.pcadv.org

The Office of Women Advocates

Box 11382
Fernandez Juancus Station
Santurce, PR 00910
(787) 721-7676 Fax: (787) 725-9248

Rhode Island Coalition Against Domestic Violence

422 Post Road, Suite 102
Warwick, RI 02888
(401) 467-9940 Fax: (401) 467-9943
(800) 494-8100 In State
Website: www.ricadv.org
Email: ricadv@ricadv.org

South Carolina Coalition Against Domestic Violence and Sexual Assault

P.O. Box 7776
Columbia, SC 29202
(803) 256-2900 Fax: (803) 256-1030
(800) 260-9293 Nationwide
Website: www.sccadvasa.org

South Dakota Coalition Against Domestic Violence & Sexual Assault

P.O. Box 141
Pierre, SD 57501
(605) 945-0869 Fax: (605) 945-0870
(800) 572-9196 Nationwide

Website: www.sdcedsv.org
Email: SKing@SDCEDSV.org

Tennessee Coalition Against Domestic and Sexual Violence

2 International Plaza Drive, Suite 425
Nashville, TN 37217
(615) 386-9406 Fax: (615) 383-2967
(800) 289-9018 In State
Website: www.tncoalition.org
Email: tcadsv@tcadsv.org

Texas Council On Family Violence

P.O. Box 163865
Austin, TX 78716
(512) 794-1133 Fax: (512) 794-1199
Website: www.tcfv.org

Utah Domestic Violence Coalition

124 South 400 East, Suite 300
Salt Lake City, UT 84111
(801) 521-5544 Fax: (801) 521-5548
Website: www.udvc.org

Women's Coalition of St. Croix

P.O. Box 222734
Christiansted
St. Croix, VI 00822
(340) 773-9272 Fax: (340) 773-9062

Website: www.wcstx.org
Email: info@wcstx.org

Vermont Network Against Domestic Violence and Sexual Assault

P.O. Box 405
Montpelier, VT 05601
(802) 223-1302 Fax: (802) 223-6943
(802) 223-1115 TTY
Website: www.vtnetwork.org
Email: vtnetwork@vtnetwork.org

Virginia Sexual & Domestic Violence Action Alliance

1118 West Main Street
Richmond, VA 23230
Office: 804.377.0335 Fax: 804.377.0339
Website: www.vsdvalliance.org
E-mail: info@vsdvalliance.org

Washington State Coalition Against Domestic Violence

711 Capitol Way, Suite 702
Olympia, WA 98501
(360) 586-1022 Fax: (360) 586-1024
(360) 586-1029 TTY

1511 Third Avenue, Suite 433
Seattle, WA 98101
(206) 389-2515 Fax: (206) 389-2520

(800) 886-2880 In State
(206) 389-2900 TTY
Website: www.wscadv.org
Email: wscadv@wscadv.org

Washington State Native American Coalition Against Domestic and Sexual Assault

P.O. Box 3937
Sequim, WA 98382
(360) 352-3120 Fax: (360) 357-3858
(888) 352-3120
Website: www.womenspirit.net

West Virginia Coalition Against Domestic Violence

5004 Elk River Road South
Elkview, WV 25071
(304) 965-3552 Fax: (304) 965-3572
Website: www.wvcadv.org
Email: website@wvcadv.org

End Domestic Abuse Wisconsin: The Wisconsin Coalition Against Domestic Violence

1245 East Washington Avenue, Suite 150
Madison, WI 53703
(608) 255-0539 Fax: (608) 255-3560
Website: www.endabusewi.org
Email: wcadv@wcadv.org

Wyoming Coalition Against Domestic Violence and Sexual Assault

P.O. Box 236
710 Garfield Street, Suite 218
Laramie, WY 82073
(307) 755-5481 Fax: (307) 755-5482
(800) 990-3877 Nationwide
Website: www.wyomingdvsa.org
Email: info@wyomingdvsa.org

A Sample Prayer

Prayer of Forgiveness

"Lord, I have unforgiveness in my heart for

_____. I know that no matter the pain they

caused me, for me to move on in my life and to be forgiven

by you, I have to forgive them. This is not an easy thing for

me to do. The hurt and pain they have caused me, I am

still healing from. I cannot do this by myself. Please give

me the strength and help me to forgive them. I pray these

things in Jesus Name."

- Tanya Smith

A Poem

Standing Tall

Breathing, looking, feeling and walking
Deciding, choosing, living and talking
Just like a developing child; an adolescent learning
Just like an endless beginning a genuine yearning

Independent, supported or alone
Beg, borrow, or maybe one day I'll even own
There is definitely a light and it is calling me
Close my eyes spread my wings and I will fly free

No more shame, pretend, cheap smiles and lies
No more ifs, buts, maybes or whys?
Who are you? What do you want? How do you sleep?
I know now I am not your possession to abuse and keep

You were right, it's dramatic, and all for show
But it was you in the lead role, so desperate to grow
Like a parasite you tried to consume and destroy my life
Like a human being I tried to be your partner, friend and
wife

Go back to where you came from; it is what you do best
Go back to being nothing,; an annoying little pest
And when you get there be sure look up high
Can you see me beaming brightly, lighting up the sky

Each night I am reminded that you are evil, selfish and vile
Each night I am reminded how lucky I am, blessed and
smile
You should see them now you've gone; happy, confident
and born again
All their own work, they erased you and survived any pain

It was much easier than I thought; you can't miss what was
never there
But unlike you, I did feel true love, I wanted to grow,
experience and share
What a waste, a pointless thought and an unwanted gift
All you saw was credibility, an excuse and blame to shift

It is getting closer, that beautiful light calling me
Close my eyes spread my wings and I am flying free
It's over, just given up and please let us be
Never again imprisoned, now and forever I'm holding the
key

Your self-pity and fairy tales fall on deaf ears
Your stories and lies create no sympathy tears
One by one everyone is hearing the truth
T.R.U.T.H. comes with real evidence and proof

I swear this is the final night you will give me no sleep
There's no master plan or cunning revenge for me to reap
You are a lonely little man, idiot, bully, gambling fool
You've lost again; tough guy but I've got it all
Do you feel small?
Pathetic and cruel
Down, down you fall
At last I am standing tall
...We've got it all

For speaking engagements or book signings please

email tanyasmithministries@gmail.com

To bring the Damaged but Not Broken Conference to your church or city, please email rejuvenatedwomensfoundation@gmail.com

Acknowledgments

Through my domestic violence relationships and my struggles there are so many friends and family to thank. I am going to take the next few minutes to thank a few. If I forgot you, please understand I did not mean to. This book has been a challenge for me emotionally and spiritually to write, but I thank God first and foremost for His love, guidance and strength.

Shonda James I wouldn't know what I would have done without you being my sister. I know most of this story we went through together and even though that is your story to tell, I know that us living the horrors together and surviving made us the best friends and sisters that we are some 28 years later. No matter the distance between us in miles and states, you are the true definition of a true friend. I love you.

Tessa Lawrence where would I be without my ride or die! You have always had my back since the fifth grade.

There is nothing time nor distance could do to separate us. You stood by my side not only once but twice through these storms and I am forever grateful. I love you Sis.

Barry Richards words cannot begin to thank you for all the love, understanding and support you have given me this last year. I don't know what I would have done without you. You have encouraged me on my hardest and toughest days to make sure that I was going to continue to stand strong and make it through the storm. You are the light in all my dark days. I love you.

Versail Roddey, my best friend, my confidant, my gym trainer and one of my biggest supporters ever! Since the day we met over twelve years ago, you have given me a shoulder to cry on more times that I can remember. You remained consistent in my life when everything was failing, and everything was changing. Thank you so much for being my rock. I love you.

Tee Thompson even though we are no longer

married you were the best friend and support system I could have ever asked for. I know that God placed you in my life even though we messed it up! But without your love, patience, and prayers the aftermath would have been so much more difficult. You would sit with me through my fears and nightmares and let me know that I was safe. No one could have done that any better than you did. Even after the divorce and we were back on speaking terms (lol), I called you after my second marriage ended because of domestic violence and once again you were there for me. Because you had seen firsthand my battles and helped me overcome before, your words of encouragement and prayers were a true blessing.

Pastors Billy and Thai Pickard thank you for helping me through this process from the first abusive relationship and believing that God would deliver and restore me. You gave me the spiritual guidance I needed to forgive and be the strong woman of God that I am.

Minister Sharon Johnson! Sister you are such a inspiration. Our spirits connected from day one. You have been my best friend, sister and strongest spiritual warfare battle partner ever! Every time I needed someone to step into the war room with me and take the devil on head on, you have always been my girl. Today I know there is no one else in the world I would call to step into the spirit realm with me. There are women waiting on you lady. Women that need to see and hear your strength. I love you.

Melissa NeSmith RWF would not have been what it is without you and for reviewing the book before anyone else!! Girlfriend you rock! You are such an inspiration to me to become better, to never settle and keep striving. To your wonderful hubby and my big, little brother Cyril, thank you for sharing her with me and for all you have done through the years to show me love and support not only personally, spiritually, but also in helping with RWF. I love you both so much and I pray God continues to bless you.

Dr. Tommy Campbell, Jr, wow we have been on this ministerial journey together since 2004! You have become one of my biggest supporters. You pray with me when I need it, you and Kellie are a big part of my life and family. No matter when any of us, including my kids, need you, you guys are there. I look forward to continuing to work ministry with you and staying great friends and family forever.

Chris King, thank you so much for the wonderful design you did on my book cover. We have known each other many years and I am glad God brought you into my spirit to work on this cover for me. I look forward to doing a lot of business with you in the future. There is so much more work to be done! Everyone please checks out his designs at his company's Facebook page Creative Design Kings and website www.creativedesignkings.com.

I saved you for last Apostle H. Sheldon McCray because we are not done yet! We have had our differences. Mainly because I was rebellious and the devil was taking me through so much during my divorce, but you never gave up on me. You never gave up on my calling, or my vision. Thank you for your covering and guidance at New Birth Sounds of Thunder Christian Center and for working ministry and RWF with me. It is such an honor to sit at your feet and to learn and grow. I am blessed to have you as my spiritual father. It's 20/20 Vision time!

And to the many friends along the way for always being there for me and having my back, I thank you.

Made in the USA
Columbia, SC
06 July 2020

12030981R00093